Crypto Airdrops: The Evolution of Free Tokens

Unlocking the Power of Community and Growth in the Cryptocurrency World

Thomas D. Urban

Copyright

© 2024 by [Thomas D. Urban]

All rights reserved. No part of this publication may be reproduced, distributed, or transmitted in any form or by any means, including photocopying, recording, or other electronic or mechanical methods, without the prior written permission of the publisher, except in the case of brief quotations embodied in critical reviews and certain other noncommercial uses permitted by copyright law.

Table of Contents

INTRODUCTION 1

CHAPTER 1 6

Understanding Airdrops 6

Meaning and Categories of Airdrops 6

The Function of Airdrops and Their Reasoning for Crypto Projects 9

The Benefits and Drawbacks of Airdrop Engagement 13

CHAPTER 2 16

The Mechanics of Claiming Airdrops 16

Registering for Projects 17

Submitting Wallet Addresses 21

Tips for Encouraging Achievement and Avoiding Fraud 23

Tools and Platforms for Finding and Monitoring Airdrops 25

CHAPTER 3 28

Popular Airdrop Projects 28

Case Studies of Successful Airdrops 31

Analysis of Airdrop Methods and Trends ... 33

CHAPTER 4 36

Legal and Fiscal Aspects to Take into Account 36

Legal and Regulatory Issues 36

Tax Implications for Airdrop Recipients 38

Requirements for Compliance and Reporting 40

CHAPTER 5 43

Future Trends and Innovations 43

New Developments in Airdrops 43

Speculation Regarding the Prospects of Airdrops 45

Forecasts for Development in Reaction to
Market Dynamics and Regulatory Shifts 47
CONCLUSION 50

INTRODUCTION

Airdrops are a fascinating phenomenon in the rapidly changing world of cryptocurrencies, providing users with the chance to obtain digital assets at no cost. This overview explores the idea of airdrops, their role in the cryptocurrency ecosystem, and a brief account of how they have changed over time.

Understanding Airdrops

When we talk about airdrops about cryptocurrencies, we mean giving away free tokens or coins to a lot of wallet addresses. Airdrops are different from traditional token distribution techniques such as initial coin offers (ICOs) or token sales, which usually require participants to purchase tokens, in that airdrops deliver tokens directly to users' wallets without requiring payment.

The importance of airdrops stems from their capacity to accomplish multiple goals at once. They are used, first and foremost, to disperse tokens to a larger audience, raising awareness of the initiative and encouraging community involvement. Second, airdrops can be a marketing tactic to create excitement about a fresh cryptocurrency project or a protocol for decentralized finance (DeFi). Projects can draw attention and encourage potential users to explore their platform or ecosystem by providing free tokens. Airdrops can also aid in bootstrapping network effects by promoting early acceptance and involvement in the ecosystem of the project.

The Development of Airdrops: A Brief Introduction

Although the idea of airdrops dates back to the early days of cryptocurrencies, it has seen substantial development. Airdrops were a very uncommon practice in the early days of the cryptocurrency business, usually carried out by tiny, community-driven initiatives as a means of giving tokens to early backers.

When the cryptocurrency Aurora coin was introduced in Iceland in 2014, it became one of the first recorded instances of airdrops. The goal of creating the Aurora coin was to provide digital currency—a type of universal basic income—to the people of Iceland. The project's goal was to provide each Icelandic citizen with a fixed quantity of Aurora coins, irrespective of their financial situation or level of involvement in the cryptocurrency market. The project attracted attention for its ambitious objectives, but it also encountered opposition and doubt about its sustainability and long-term profitability.

As the cryptocurrency space developed and gained traction, airdrops became a popular tactic used by both well-established organizations and fresh companies. Airdrops became more widespread as ICOs proliferated in the years after the Bitcoin boom as a means for ventures to stand out and garner attention in a crowded market.

Airdrops are a particularly common tactic in the DeFi area, where they are used to drive user engagement, incentivize involvement in governance systems, and jumpstart liquidity in recent years. Tokens are frequently distributed by DeFi protocols to users who engage in yield farming, stake tokens in liquidity pools, or supply liquidity to decentralized exchanges (DEXs). Utilizing these airdrops, people are rewarded for their contributions to the ecosystem, and governance tokens are distributed.

Airdrops have become a well-known aspect of the cryptocurrency scene, providing users with the chance to obtain digital assets for no cost and acting as an effective means of project promotion and community building. Airdrops have changed significantly over time, from their modest origins as a specialized distribution technique to their current position as a commonly used tactic for encouraging adoption and engagement. Airdrops are probably going to stay a vital component of the ecosystem, helping to drive development, liquidity, and participation as the cryptocurrency sector innovates and changes.

CHAPTER 1

Understanding Airdrops

Airdrops are a well-liked and innovative method for companies to disperse tokens to a broad audience in the fast-paced and dynamic world of cryptocurrency. The complexities of airdrops will be thoroughly examined in this chapter, along with their definition, different varieties, mechanisms, and justification for use. We will also look at the benefits and drawbacks of airdrops, highlighting the opportunities and difficulties they pose for cryptocurrency aficionados.

Meaning and Categories of Airdrops

Airdrops are uninvited cryptocurrency tokens or coin releases that are usually given away for free to a large number of wallet addresses. These distributions accomplish many goals, including as raising project awareness, growing the user base, and promoting trade. There are various kinds of airdrops, and each has special qualities of its own:

Holder Airdrops: A prearranged snapshot time is used to automatically distribute tokens to users who possess a particular cryptocurrency in their wallets. The purpose of these airdrops is to reward current token holders and encourage them to keep holding the money. NEM, ARDR, Stellar Lumens, and Byte Ball are a few examples of holder airdrops.

Bounty Airdrops: In exchange for tokens, users are encouraged to carry out certain activities or actions through bounty airdrops. Usually, these assignments require using social media, such as joining Telegram groups, retweeting content, or taking part in online forums. Projects can raise their profile and generate interest in their offerings by using bounty airdrops.

Retroactive Airdrops: Also referred to as retroactive awards or retroactive distributes, retroactive airdrops include giving tokens to people who have previously used a specific platform or protocol. These airdrops, which attempt to reward early adopters or active participants, are frequently based on past data or user action. Retroactive airdrops include those carried out by Furucombo, Uniswap, dYdX, and Instadapp.

NFT Airdrops: Users receive one-of-a-kind, non-transferable tokens as part of non-fungible token (NFT) airdrops. Usually, these tokens are used to denote ownership of tangible or digital goods, including virtual real estate, artwork, or collectibles. NFT airdrops have become more and more common in recent years as a means for creators and artists to thank their fans and spread the word about their work.

Exclusive Airdrops: Airdrops that are organized and hosted by particular platforms or groups are known as exclusive airdrops. To participate in these airdrops, users might need to fulfill specific requirements or conditions, such as subscribing to a newsletter, finishing a KYC verification process, or possessing a minimum quantity of tokens. Participants in exclusive airdrops frequently receive greater benefits or special possibilities.

The Function of Airdrops and Their Reasoning for Crypto Projects

Depending on the kind of airdrop and the goals of the issuing project, airdrop mechanics change.

Still, the following phases are usually involved in the basic process:

Project Preparation: The project team decides on the objectives and specifics of the airdrop, such as the total amount of tokens to be given out, participant eligibility requirements, and mode of distribution.

Snapshot or Activity Tracking: The project records the holdings or activity of qualified users by taking a snapshot of the blockchain at a particular block height or timestamp for holder airdrops and retroactive airdrops. Users must carry out specific tasks or actions to get bounty airdrops; these actions are monitored and confirmed by the project staff.

Token Distribution: The project gives the tokens to qualified participants after the snapshot or activity tracking is finished. For holder and retroactive airdrops, this distribution can happen automatically; for bounty airdrops, it might need to be manually verified and approved.

Claiming or Redemption: To claim or redeem their tokens, bounty airdrop participants may be required to submit their wallet addresses or carry out further verification procedures. Tokens for both retroactive and holder airdrops are normally sent straight into participants' wallets.

Crypto projects run airdrops for many reasons, many of which are related to their aims and objectives. The following are a few typical justifications for airdrops:

Increasing Visibility: Airdrops assist projects in becoming more visible and drawing the interest of possible partners, investors, and users. Projects can generate interest and buzz around their offers by extensively distributing their tokens.

Growing User Base: By delivering tokens to a large number of people, airdrops let projects quickly grow their user base. In addition to generating a lively and interested community around the project, this can aid in bootstrapping network effects.

Encouraging Trading Activity: By giving users, a reason to purchase, sell, or keep tokens, airdrops might encourage trading activity. To promote trade and liquidity provision on cryptocurrency exchanges, initiatives can distribute tokens to current token holders or active players.

Contributors: Airdrops give projects a way to thank ardent backers, early adopters, and active contributors. Through token distribution to those who have helped the project succeed, communities can be encouraged to be kind and devoted to one another.

The Benefits and Drawbacks of Airdrop Engagement

For cryptocurrency fans, there are many possible benefits to participating in airdrops, such as:

Free Token Access: Airdrops give users the chance to obtain free tokens without having to make a financial investment. As a result, people can diversify the cryptocurrencies they own and take advantage of fresh opportunities without taking a financial risk.

Prospect for Profit: If the issuing project is successful and widely adopted, airdropped coins may see a rise in value over time. Participants may be able to make substantial profits by hanging onto airdropped tokens if their value increases.

Community Involvement: Airdrops frequently include social media activities and community involvement, which can facilitate connections with like-minded enthusiasts and greater engagement with initiatives. The whole airdropping experience can be improved by this feeling of community.

However, participating in airdrops also comes with certain disadvantages and risks, including:

Fraud & Scams: Airdrops are only one example of the many fraudulent schemes and scams that exist in the Bitcoin ecosystem. Participants should use caution and perform comprehensive due diligence to prevent falling for phishing or fraud.

Opportunity Cost: Time and effort are needed to participate in airdrops, particularly in bounty programs that entail social media duties or other activities. It is recommended that participants take into account the opportunity cost of their time and assess whether the prospective benefits outweigh the expenditure of their resources.

Regulatory Uncertainty: In countries with stringent tax or securities laws, airdrops may provide legal and regulatory challenges. It is recommended that participants acquaint themselves with the pertinent rules and regulations within their jurisdiction and, if required, obtain expert guidance.

Understanding the dynamic and ever-changing cryptocurrency market requires a grasp of airdrops. People can decide for themselves whether or not to take part in these unusual and cutting-edge distribution methods by learning about the definitions, kinds, physics, and reasoning behind airdrops. While free tokens and community involvement are two possible advantages of airdrops, there are hazards and difficulties that users should carefully evaluate before participating.

CHAPTER 2

The Mechanics of Claiming Airdrops

We'll get into the specifics of claiming airdrops in this chapter, giving readers a thorough overview of navigating the world of free cryptocurrency tokens. There are multiple phases involved in claiming airdrops: signing up for projects, finishing social media assignments, and sending wallet addresses. We'll also go over ways to maximize profits and reduce your chance of falling for con artists. Furthermore, we will go into the several instruments and systems accessible for identifying and monitoring airdrops, enabling readers to fully capitalize on this profitable prospect.

Registering for Projects

The first step in claiming an airdrop is to identify eligible projects and register for participation. Many cryptocurrency projects conduct airdrops to promote their tokens and engage with the community. To register for an airdrop, follow these steps:

Research: Begin researching forthcoming airdrops and selecting projects that fit your investment objectives and areas of interest. Airdrops are listed in a curated manner on websites such as airdrops.io and airdropalert.com, which also include comprehensive project details.

Project Website: Go to the project's official website to learn more about the airdrop. Seek out a specific announcement or page that outlines the conditions of the airdrop and the registration procedure. Observe the eligibility requirements, as certain airdrops might only be available in a particular area or require a certain set of activities to be eligible.

Registration Form: Fill out any required registration forms or provide the necessary information to participate in the airdrop. This may include your email address, social media profiles, and cryptocurrency wallet addresses. Be cautious when sharing personal information and ensure that you are using secure, reputable platforms.

Verification: To stop fraud and abuse, some projects could need proof of your identity or the ownership of particular cryptocurrencies. If you need to finish the verification process, just follow the guidelines that the project team has given you.

Confirmation: The project team ought to send you a confirmation email or notification as soon as your airdrop registration has been approved. You might need this information later on to claim your prizes, so keep it close to hand.

Completing Social Media Tasks

Many airdrops require participants to complete social media tasks to earn tokens. These tasks typically involve activities such as following the project on Twitter, joining their Telegram group, liking their Facebook page, or sharing promotional posts. Here's how to navigate social media tasks for airdrops:

Task Requirements: Review the airdrop instructions carefully to understand the specific social media tasks required to qualify for rewards. Make note of any deadlines or additional conditions associated with each task.

Engagement: Actively engage with the project's social media channels by liking, commenting, and sharing relevant posts. This not only increases your chances of earning tokens but also helps to build community awareness and support for the project.

Tracking: Keep track of your progress and ensure that you have completed all required tasks before the deadline. Some projects may use tracking tools or require participants to submit proof of completion, such as screenshots or links to shared posts.

Quality over Quantity: Focus on quality engagement rather than simply fulfilling the minimum requirements. Genuine interactions with the project and its community are more likely to be rewarded and contribute to the success of the airdrop campaign.

Submitting Wallet Addresses

Once you have completed the necessary registration and social media tasks, you'll need to submit your cryptocurrency wallet addresses to receive your airdrop rewards. Here's how to safely submit your wallet addresses:

Wallet Selection: To keep your airdrop tokens safe, pick a reliable and suitable cryptocurrency wallet. Mobile wallets, desktop wallets, and hardware wallets are common choices. Make that the tokens being given in the airdrop are compatible with the wallet you have selected.

Wallet Security: Take safety measures to safeguard your private keys and keep your wallet safe. Make sure to activate two-factor authentication, create secure passwords, and save your private keys offline whenever you can. Don't give anyone access to your secret keys or sensitive data.

Submission Procedure: Send in your wallet addresses for the airdrop by following the guidelines the project team provides. This might include submitting wallet addresses via social media, completing a form on the project website, or interacting with a smart contract.

Verification: You might need to provide proof of ownership or confirm that you are taking part in the airdrop after inputting your wallet addresses. This can be using your wallet address to sign a message or completing further identity verification procedures.

Confirmation: The project team should send you a confirmation as soon as your wallet addresses have been successfully submitted and checked. Since airdrop prizes are usually sent straight to participant wallets, keep a watch out for any incoming transactions in your wallet.

Tips for Encouraging Achievement and Avoiding Fraud

Despite the potential for financial gain, taking part in airdrops requires caution and diligence to prevent falling for con artists or fraudulent operations. The following advice can help you safeguard yourself and maximize rewards:

Research: Before taking part in their airdrops, thoroughly investigate the projects. Seek out details regarding the project's technology, team, roadmap, and community support. Steer clear of projects that provide ambiguous or deceptive information as they can be bogus.

Verify Official Channels: When registering for airdrops or finishing tasks, only engage with official project channels and websites. To fool participants into donating money or divulging sensitive information, scammers frequently pose as authentic enterprises.

Preserve Your Privacy: Exercise caution while providing sensitive or personal information to projects or outside websites. When communicating, try to stay away from giving more information than is required and use secure channels.

Watch Out for Phishing Attempts: Be on the lookout for emails or URLs that seem fishy or that seem to be from the people organizing an airdrop. Never click on strange links or download attachments from unidentified sources. Instead, confirm the legitimacy of communications by visiting the official project channels and websites.

Keep Up: Keep up with the most recent advancements and trends in the cryptocurrency world, such as modifications to regulations, dangers to security, and the best ways to take advantage of airdrops. Participate in online forums and groups to meet new people and exchange ideas.

Tools and Platforms for Finding and Monitoring Airdrops

It might be difficult to find and follow airdrops because there are so many projects and campaigns in the bitcoins industry. Thankfully, there are several resources and platforms accessible to assist you in maintaining organization and knowledge. Here are a few well-liked choices:

Airdrop Aggregator Websites: Websites like airdrops.io, airdropalert.com, and coinairdrops.com aggregate information about upcoming and ongoing airdrops, providing detailed descriptions, eligibility criteria, and registration instructions. These platforms often include user-friendly interfaces and filtering options to help you find airdrops that match your preferences.

Telegram Channels: Many cryptocurrency projects and airdrop communities maintain Telegram channels dedicated to sharing information about airdrops and bounty campaigns. Joining these channels allows you to receive real-time updates, participate in discussions, and connect with other participants.

Social Media Groups: Information and networking possibilities can be found in Facebook groups, Twitter accounts, and Reddit forums devoted to Bitcoin airdrops. You may communicate with like-minded people, exchange ideas, and find fresh airdrop chances by joining these communities.

Apps for Tracking Airdrops: You can keep track of airdrops and manage your participation with the help of mobile apps such as CoinMarketCap and Airdrop Alert. These applications offer portfolio management features, alerts about fresh airdrops, and interaction with well-known.

CHAPTER 3

Popular Airdrop Projects

Airdropping cryptocurrency has grown in popularity as a marketing tactic for blockchain organizations looking to get more exposure, draw in more users, and provide tokens to more people. This chapter will include an analysis of case studies of successful airdrops, a look at some of the most well-known cryptocurrency projects that have carried out airdrops, and a look at trends and approaches for spotting opportunities in the airdrop market.

The Ethereum network (ETH)

The second-largest cryptocurrency by market capitalization, Ethereum, is arguably one of the most well-known instances of a project that has carried out a profitable airdrop. Ethereum held a pre-sale of its Ether (ETH) tokens in 2014 to raise money for the advancement of its blockchain technology. Ethereum gave pre-sale participants extra tokens as a thank-you for being early backers via an airdrop.

An important part of creating a community around the project and igniting interest among early adopters was the Ethereum airdrop. Additionally, it contributed to the broad distribution of ETH tokens, which established the groundwork for Ethereum's network of smart contracts and decentralized applications (dApps).

Stellar Lumens (XLM)

Stellar Lumens, a blockchain platform designed for cross-border payments and asset transfers, is another notable example of a project that has leveraged airdrops to grow its user base. In 2017, the Stellar Development Foundation announced a series of airdrops to distribute free XLM tokens to holders of Bitcoin (BTC). The goal was to encourage Bitcoin users to explore the Stellar network and its features, such as fast and low-cost transactions.

The Stellar airdrop succeeded in attracting attention to the project and increasing the adoption of its native cryptocurrency. It also introduced many new users to the concept of blockchain-based financial services and decentralized exchanges.

EOS (EOS)

EOS is a blockchain platform known for its scalability and support for decentralized applications. In 2018, EOS conducted one of the largest airdrops in cryptocurrency history as part of its token distribution process. Throughout a year-long ICO (initial coin offering), EOS distributed tokens to investors in weekly batches.

The EOS airdrop was designed to ensure widespread distribution of tokens and to incentivize participation in the EOS ecosystem. By distributing tokens to a large number of holders, EOS aimed to create a diverse and engaged community of users and developers.

Case Studies of Successful Airdrops

Uniswap (UNI): Uniswap, a decentralized exchange (DEX) protocol built on Ethereum, conducted a highly successful retroactive airdrop in 2020. The Uniswap team distributed free UNI tokens to users who had interacted with the protocol by trading or providing liquidity before a certain date. The airdrop was intended to reward early supporters of Uniswap and to align incentives among users of the platform.

The Uniswap airdrop had a significant impact on the project's adoption and token value. It led to a surge in trading activity on the Uniswap platform and contributed to a rapid appreciation in the price of UNI tokens. Many users who received UNI tokens as part of the airdrop saw substantial returns on their investment, further driving interest in the protocol.

Chain-link (LINK): Chain-link, a decentralized oracle network that provides real-world data to smart contracts on the blockchain, conducted a series of strategic airdrops to bootstrap its ecosystem and incentivize participation from developers and data providers. By distributing free LINK tokens to users who contributed to the development and adoption of the Chain-link network, the project was able to build a robust and diverse community of stakeholders.

The Chain-link airdrops played a crucial role in establishing the project as a leader in the decentralized oracle space. They helped to attract talented developers, secure partnerships with leading blockchain projects, and drive the adoption of Chain Link's technology across various industries.

Analysis of Airdrop Methods and Trends

focused Distribution: To target audiences and increase impact, a lot of successful airdrops use focused distribution techniques. Through token distribution, projects can effectively target individuals who are likely to be interested in their project and its features, such as holders of particular cryptocurrencies or users of particular platforms.

Incentive Alignment: Airdrops are often used to align incentives among stakeholders and encourage participation in a project's ecosystem. By rewarding users for contributing value to the network, projects can foster a sense of ownership and commitment among their community members.

Community Building: By allowing projects to interact with their audience and develop a devoted following, airdrops can be extremely effective tools for community building. Projects can interact with possible users, get feedback, and create connections through airdrop campaigns that may result in long-term success and growth.

Value Proposition: Efficient airdrops frequently provide users with a distinct value proposition, such as the ability to participate in a project with the potential to change the world, gain access to special features, or obtain free tokens. Communities are more likely to be interested in and participate in projects that provide attractive incentives and convey their value proposition.

All things considered, airdrops are still a well-liked and successful tactic for cryptocurrency companies trying to build their communities, promote their platforms, and increase token and ecosystem acceptance. Through the examination of thriving airdrop initiatives, trend analysis, and prospect identification, investors and enthusiasts can strategically align themselves to leverage the potential benefits and expansion prospects afforded by airdrops within the Bitcoin domain.

CHAPTER 4

Legal and Fiscal Aspects to Take into Account

It can be difficult to navigate the legal and tax landscape in the fast-paced world of cryptocurrencies, where innovation frequently outpaces regulation, especially when it comes to airdrops. With an emphasis on the US, this chapter will examine the legal and regulatory concerns related to airdrops. We will also discuss the tax ramifications for recipients of airdrops and guide on compliance and reporting obligations.

Legal and Regulatory Issues

Airdrops exist in a legal gray area, as regulators around the world grapple with how to classify and regulate these distributions of free tokens. In the United States, the Securities and Exchange Commission (SEC) plays a central role in overseeing the cryptocurrency market and determining whether certain tokens qualify as securities under existing securities laws.

One of the key considerations in determining the regulatory status of airdrops is whether the tokens being distributed meet the criteria for securities. According to the Howey Test, a legal standard established by the Supreme Court, an asset is considered a security if it involves an investment of money in a common enterprise with the expectation of profits solely from the efforts of others. If a token meets these criteria, it may be classified as a security and subject to securities laws.

However, not all tokens distributed through airdrops are necessarily securities. Some airdrops involve the distribution of utility tokens, which are designed to provide access to a specific product or service within a blockchain ecosystem. Utility tokens may not meet the criteria for securities and therefore may be subject to different regulatory treatment.

Despite the lack of clear guidance from regulators, cryptocurrency projects conducting airdrops should proceed with caution and seek legal advice to ensure compliance with relevant securities laws. Failure to do so could result in regulatory scrutiny and potential enforcement actions.

Tax Implications for Airdrop Recipients

Recipients of airdrops should be mindful of the tax ramifications of obtaining free tokens in addition to legal issues. There are still numerous unsolved problems regarding the Internal Revenue Service's (IRS) sparse instructions on how to classify airdrops for tax purposes.

Determining the value of tokens obtained via an airdrop is a crucial problem. Recipients of airdrops could have to rely on the tokens' fair market value at the time of receipt if the IRS doesn't provide clear guidelines. Determining this can be difficult, especially for tokens with minimal liquidity or those that are not yet listed on exchanges.

After the tokens' value is established, airdrop recipients need to decide if receiving the tokens is a capital gain or taxable income. How tokens are treated may vary depending on many circumstances, such as the recipient's intentions at the time of receipt and whether or not they are seen as gifts or as compensation for service.

Tokens obtained through airdrops may generally be taxable as ordinary income at their fair market value if they are deemed to represent payment for services done. However, if the tokens are obtained without any expectation of compensation, they can be regarded as capital assets and be liable to capital gains tax upon exchange or sale.

Requirements for Compliance and Reporting

Recipients of airdrops are in charge of paying their taxes and informing the IRS of any taxable events. This could entail paying any applicable taxes on the value of the tokens received and declaring the receipt of tokens as income on their yearly tax filings.

Airdrop beneficiaries should be aware of any potential reporting requirements to the Financial

Crimes Enforcement Network (FinCEN) or other regulatory bodies in addition to tax reporting requirements. Anti-money laundering (AML) and know-your-customer (KYC) requirements apply to cryptocurrency transactions, and recipients may be required to declare specific transactions or holdings if they reach specific criteria.

Recipients of airdrops should also keep thorough records of all their cryptocurrency transactions, including information about the airdrops they have taken part in and the worth of the tokens they have been given. This will support maintaining adherence to legal and regulatory obligations and offer supporting documents in the event of an audit or tax authorities' investigation.

Airdrops bring special legal and financial issues for both receivers and cryptocurrency projects. Participants should proceed with caution and seek professional assistance to guarantee compliance with applicable laws and regulations, even while regulators continue to struggle with how to categorize and control airdrops. Through comprehension of the tax and regulatory ramifications of airdrops, participants may reduce risks and confidently traverse the constantly changing cryptocurrency terrain.

CHAPTER 5

Future Trends and Innovations

Airdrops have played a crucial role in the development of cryptocurrencies, progressing from straightforward freebies to intricate marketing and distribution plans. This chapter will examine the new trends in airdrops, forecast how they might alter in reaction to market conditions and legislative changes, and speculate on their potential place in the Bitcoin ecosystem.

New Developments in Airdrops

Retroactive Airdrops: In recent years, retroactive airdrops have become increasingly popular, especially in the DeFi domain. Retroactive airdrops give tokens to users based on their previous interactions with a protocol, in contrast to traditional airdrops that reward users for their participation or future activities. This method has been pioneered by projects like Uniswap and dYdX, which retrospectively award early users with governance tokens. As DeFi protocols work to encourage early uptake and user engagement, this tendency is probably going to keep happening.

NFT Airdrops: The digitization of art, collectibles, and other unique assets has led to an explosion in the adoption of non-fungible tokens (NFTs). In response, to raise awareness and encourage new users, certain projects and artists have started to airdrop NFTs. By giving receivers access to unique digital items, these NFT airdrops instill a sense of worth and scarcity. We should anticipate additional projects trying with this type of airdrop as the NFT market grows.

Exclusive Airdrops: Hosted and run by websites such as airdrops.io, exclusive airdrops give players access to special chances that aren't open to the general public. Cryptocurrency aficionados highly prize these airdrops since they frequently include excellent projects and large incentives. Through collaborating on respectable projects and carrying out extensive due research, platforms can provide users with worthwhile income prospects while upholding their reputation and credibility in the community.

Speculation Regarding the Prospects of Airdrops

Shortly, airdrops are expected to become more and more significant in the cryptocurrency ecosystem. Here are some conjectural predictions for their future:

Improved User Acquisition and Engagement: Airdrops will remain effective instruments for attracting new users and interacting with current ones. Projects can gain traction, create a sense of community, and encourage platform and token adoption by providing incentives for involvement. As the competition in the cryptocurrency field heats up, airdrops will be a crucial part of growth and marketing plans.

Integration with DeFi and NFTs: In line with broader trends in the cryptocurrency industry, airdrops will be more tightly integrated with decentralized finance (DeFi) protocols and non-fungible tokens (NFTs). It is anticipated that airdrops will be utilized to reward early contributors and supporters with rare and valuable NFTs, as well as to promote liquidity-providing, yield farming, and other DeFi operations.

Personalized and Targeted Airdrops: As blockchain technology develops, airdrops will get more specialized and customized, catering to the unique inclinations and interests of each user. Projects may find and reward users who are most likely to add value to their ecosystems by utilizing data analytics and machine learning algorithms. This makes resource allocation more effective and increases user engagement.

Forecasts for Development in Reaction to Market Dynamics and Regulatory Shifts

The future development of airdrops will surely be shaped by changes in regulations and market forces. Here are some hypotheses regarding potential responses from airdrops:

Compliance and Transparency: To reduce legal risks and foster user trust, airdrops must give compliance and transparency a priority as regulatory scrutiny grows. Strong KYC (Know Your Customer) and AML (Anti-Money Laundering) protocols will be implemented as part of projects to guarantee that airdrop recipients are eligible and authentic following relevant laws and regulations.

Move Towards Permissioned Airdrops: We might witness a move towards permissioned airdrops, in which users must choose to participate and meet specific requirements, to allay worries about tax responsibility and regulatory ambiguity. Projects can assure regulatory compliance and steer clear of potential legal hazards related to unsolicited distributions by using this strategy.

Market-driven Distribution Models: The planning and implementation of airdrops will be influenced by market factors including shifts in investor mood and variations in token values. In reaction to market conditions, projects may modify their distribution strategies. Tokens are carefully distributed to optimize impact and reduce value dilution for current holders.

Airdrops are positioned to keep developing as an adaptable and dynamic method for interacting with users, distributing tokens, and promoting ecosystem growth for cryptocurrencies. Projects can use airdrops to accomplish their strategic goals and open up new avenues for innovation and value generation by embracing emerging trends, adjusting to regulatory changes, and responding to market dynamics.

CONCLUSION

Taking Advantage of the Airdrop Economy

We highlight the most important discoveries and lessons learned from our investigation into the airdrop business in this last chapter. While stressing the value of caution and due investigation in navigating this ever-changing terrain, we invite readers to think about airdrops as a possible source of passive income and investment opportunities.

Summary of Key Findings

In this book, we have explored the nuances of airdrops, from their inception to their development as a well-known tactic used by cryptocurrency projects to interact with their communities. The following are the main conclusions we have drawn:

Airdrop Definition and Types: Airdrops encompass various distribution methods, including holder airdrops, bounty airdrops, retroactive airdrops, NFT airdrops, and exclusive airdrops. Each type offers unique opportunities and challenges for participants.

Mechanics of Claiming Airdrops: Participating in airdrops involves completing specific tasks, such as joining social media channels, reposting content, or holding certain cryptocurrencies in designated wallets. Understanding the process and following best practices can help maximize rewards and avoid scams.

Well-known Airdrop Projects: To foster their communities and boost token acceptance, many well-known cryptocurrency projects have successfully carried out airdrops. Analyzing case studies of previous airdrops can give important insights into how they affect the value of tokens and project growth.

Legal and Tax Considerations: Participants in airdrops need to be mindful of the legal and regulatory ramifications, particularly concerning potential tax obligations. To prevent future legal problems, reporting obligations must be followed, as well as applicable legislation.

Future Innovations and Trends: The airdrop industry is always changing, and new ideas like exclusive airdrops, NFT airdrops, and retroactive airdrops are becoming more and more popular. Staying up to date with these advancements will assist investors in recognizing bright spots within the developing airdrop market.

Embracing Airdrops as Opportunities

As we conclude our exploration of the airdrop economy, we want to emphasize the potential benefits of participating in airdrops as a means of earning passive income and exploring investment opportunities. Airdrops offer several advantages for both cryptocurrency projects and participants:

Portfolio Diversification: Airdrops let investors spread out their Bitcoin holdings without having to make extra financial investments. People can discover new projects and obtain new tokens without jeopardizing their money by taking part in airdrops.

Community Engagement: To interact with their communities and encourage user participation, bitcoin projects might use airdrops as an effective strategy. Investors can become a part of lively communities and help great projects flourish by actively engaging in airdrops.

Possibility of Value Appreciation: Airdropped tokens could see an increase in value over time, particularly if the underlying project succeeds and gathers traction. Shrewd investors who spot good ventures early on can make substantial returns on their investment by holding airdropped tokens.

Passive Income Generation: Participants in airdrops can generate passive income by holding specified cryptocurrencies or by executing easy tasks, which will award them tokens. People can earn steady income streams and acquire tokens over time by strategically participating and planning.

Sustaining Attention and Exertion

Even though airdrops offer thrilling chances, players must be cautious and perform their research before taking part in any airdrop activity.

The following are some important things to remember:

Scam Awareness: There are many frauds and scams in the Bitcoin world, including phony airdrops intended to trick gullible users. It is imperative to confirm the authenticity of airdrop initiatives and use caution when exchanging personal information or communicating with unidentified parties.

Risk management: Airdrops come with many intrinsic hazards, such as the possibility of token devaluation, project failure, or legal issues. To minimize possible losses, investors should evaluate the risk-reward profile of each airdrop opportunity and deploy their resources appropriately.

Regulatory Compliance: Careful thought must be given to the regulatory ambiguity surrounding airdrops, especially concerning potential tax ramifications and legal requirements. To ensure compliance with legal obligations, participants should familiarize themselves with pertinent rules and, if necessary, obtain expert guidance.

Long-Term Strategy: An individual's financial objectives and long-term investment strategy should be in line with their participation in airdrops. Although airdrops might yield immediate benefits, investors want to evaluate a project's durability and possible lifespan before allocating resources.

Concluding Remarks

As we draw to a close our examination of the airdrop economy, we implore readers to view airdrops as an excellent chance to add variety to their cryptocurrency holdings, interact with creative initiatives, and maybe generate passive income. In the ever-changing world of cryptocurrencies, investors may successfully navigate the airdrop landscape and seize opportunities for financial development by remaining informed, being cautious, and performing rigorous due diligence.

www.ingramcontent.com/pod-product-compliance
Lightning Source LLC
Chambersburg PA
CBHW071217240526
45470CB00018B/2062